I0462704

# 7 Irrefutable Steps to GREAT Credit!

## *Credit Repair in a Nutshell*

### Money Back Guarantee!

7 Irrefutable Steps to GREAT Credit provides numerous and proven techniques to restore and repair your credit report. Moreover, we pride ourselves on assuring your satisfaction in building a better financial future. That is why we make a Money Back Guarantee.

If your credit score does not improve after nine months of implementing and using the techniques within this publication, send a copy of your initial FICO score, your score reflected nine months after your initial FICO score, a copy of the dispute forms and techniques used, along with this publication and receipt of purchase. Before sending materials, e-mail armlaw1@juno.com and inform us of your decisions. We will issue a confirmation number.

# Table of Contents

**Step 1: Order Your Credit Reports**

The three credit bureaus are record keepers. They sell information to lenders, insurance companies, and employers for profit. Credit bureaus *only* confirm the information in your credit report if you make a request.

You must order your credit reports from all three bureaus at:

www.AnnualCreditReport.com Or by calling 877-322-8228. The contact information for the individual credit bureaus is:

Equifax Information Services LLC
P.O. Box 740256
Atlanta, GA 30374
800-685-1111
www.equifax.com

Experian
P.O. Box 2002
Allen TX 75013-3742
888-397-3742
www.experian.com

TransUnion
P.O. Box 2000
Chester, PA 19022-2000
800-888-4213
www.transunion.com

Upon request, the credit bureaus are required to provide you with one free copy of your credit report every year. If you have been denied credit, employment, or housing, you are also entitled to an additional free credit report.

If you are not eligible to receive a free credit report, you should pay for the report. However, do not purchase a "3-in-1" merged or use a mortgage "tri-merge" credit report. A merged report does not provide enough data to effectively repair your credit.

Although the reports do not provide the credit scores, you should purchase them at www.myfico.com/12 .

**Note:**
1. Do not tell the credit bureaus that you are repairing your credit. The law provides credit bureaus with loopholes, which can hurt your attempts at credit repair.
2. If you dispute everything at one time, the credit bureaus will suspect you are attempting credit repair. Thus do not dispute more than three items at a time.
3. Wait at least 60 days before attempting to dispute additional items.
4. Challenge the items that are doing the most damage, first (for example, collections, charge offs, write offs).
5. Challenge items that are late 60 days or more.

**Step 2: Analyze and Review**

Once you received your credit reports, make two copies of every page. Keep the original for your files. Take notes on the first copy. Submit the second copy with your disputes. If you do not understand the data in your credit report, call the credit bureau. They are required by law to assist you.

The five major categories to your credit report are:

## 1. Personal Information

Examine the accuracy of the basic information. For example, check to see whether your name, previous/current address, social security number, or birth date is correct.

## 2. Public Records

Bankruptcies, judgments, arrests, child support issues, liens, and garnishments, are usually in the public records section of a credit report.

## 3. Credit Items

Included in your credit report is a complete list of all companies that claim to have given you credit. The list will include the account number, the name of the creditor, the current balance, the monthly payment, the numbers of times you have been 30, 60 or 90 days late, and the account status.

Ensure that the names and accuracy of past-due amounts and balances are correct. Check also the accuracy of the "date of last activity" (DLA). If your account has been transferred to a collection agency, look for *duplicate accounts*.

## 4. Inquiries

Your Fico credit score can be damaged if there are many recent inquiries in your credit report. Thus, do not apply to numerous companies for credit. If you are looking to buy a car or finance a large purchase, find the best rate and price before applying for financing.

## 5. FICO Credit Scores

Your FICO credit score is a 3-digit number ranging from 300-850. Arguably, your credit score matters more than your annual salary and your net worth. Your ultimate goal is to receive a score of 720 or above. After you receive a 720 average credit score, lenders often compete to offer you the best interest rates.

Aforementioned, you can receive your FICO scores at www.myfico.com/12 . The best time to receive your FICO scores is 60 to 90 days before a major purchase. Give yourself time to fix errors to get the terms and rate you need. If you want an idea where your score range is, go to: www.bankrate.com/brm/fico/calc.asp. Once you know your score, you can use the loan calculator at www.increaseyourcreditscores.com/savemoney .

Many financial institutions and loan officers refer to credit scores as "FICO SCORES". The credit bureaus use software developed by Fair Isaac Company (FICO) to analyze all of your credit rating with a single score. Experian calls its credit score the "FICO Risk Model", TransUnion calls its credit score "FICO Classic", and Equifax calls its credit score "Beacon".

Remember that the FICO score is the most important information in your credit report. If your score is 720 or more, you have very good credit. If your score is 670 or more, your credit is good. If your score is less than 600, you have to work on building your credit. Please note that your scores change only when the data used to calculate the credit scores change. The following are the factors that affect your FICO score:

1. Payment History (35%)
    a. Delinquencies
    b. Bankruptcies, liens or judgments
    c. Length of time since last delinquency
2. The Amount of Money You Owe (30%)
    a. Total amount owed
    b. Not enough, or too many, credit cards
    c. The relationship of your balance in comparison to the credit limit (keep your credit card under 30 percent of your credit limit)
3. Length of Time of Credit History (15%)
    a. Average age of accounts
    b. Length of time since the account was opened

4. Amount of New Credit Requested (10%)
    a. Inquiries made (If you have seven related car purchasing inquiries within a short period of time, the credit bureaus know you are rate shopping. Thus, do your shopping for a car loan or mortgage within a 14-day period because all car loans or mortgages within this time period count as only one credit inquiry.)
    b. Number of new accounts
    c. Time since last account opened
5. The Type of Credit (10%)
    a. The amount of finance-company accounts
    b. The number of revolving accounts versus installment accounts (If you really want the highest possible score, do not use your revolving accounts for 60 days after you have paid them off.)

## Step 3: Removing Negative Information

*Never dispute items online* because you may have to agree to the terms and conditions of the credit bureau online, which may waive your rights to dispute an item again if it is verified online. Thus, submit your credit disputes through a fax or regular mail.

Before getting started, create three separate records for your credit bureau disputes. Keep a *copy of everything* that you submit and receive. It is important that you keep good records. Write a journal which denotes the time, date, name of contact, and the description of activity of everything that you do. If you need to go to small claims court, this journal will assist you in defending your creditors' rights.

Initially, use the dispute forms provided by the credit bureaus and check off the boxes "Not Mine" or "Not Late". Some disputes may require you to write detailed letters to support the claims.

1. Although credit inquiries are your enemy, they do not have a large impact on your credit score. Thus, do not spend a lot of time disputing them.
2. Bankruptcies can be removed after 10 years. However, if an item is more than seven years old, tell the credit bureaus to remove the items because it is obsolete.
3. If an account was paid off, but was past due, do not request to remove the account.

Tell the credit bureau that the account was never late.

4. If an account was a charged off or a collection account, write that this is **not your account** and request for the item to be removed.

5. Write all of your letters by hand and fill in the credit bureaus' dispute forms.

After you make a dispute, request an updated credit report from each bureau. Also send the dispute forms and letters to the credit bureau by certified and return receipt mail. File the return receipt and the receipt from the certified payment. If the credit bureau fails to comply with Federal laws, this will be your proof in small claims court.

According to the Fair Credit Reporting Act, when a consumer disputes information within his credit report, the credit bureau must verify the accuracy of the information within thirty days. If this information is not verified within 30 days by the credit bureau, the data must be removed or modified.

Further evidence notes that creditors also do not have the staff, or proper records, to verify consumer data within 30 days. Even if the negative information is correct and the creditors fail to reply within 30 days, the credit bureau must remove the information. **Thus, use the law to your advantage!**

*Older items* are usually easier to remove because creditors are less alarmed by older accounts that were closed or charged off. As a result, creditors are less likely to spend the time or money to verify older accounts. Accounts that were past due but are now paid off are also easy for the same aforementioned reason.

Items that are **currently in collections** or are currently past due are difficult to remove because they are active records in the creditor's report. As a result, the creditors' seek to verify these items because it is their intention to collect income from these accounts. However, you should give these items a try in your later series of disputes.

**Liens, judgments and bankruptcy** are also very difficult to dispute. Do not dispute these items until they are four years old. The credit bureaus hire people to monitor data that is released from the court. Generally, most legal records are archived after three years, and personnel are usually not paid to monitor the data, after the third year. Also, use caution with tax liens. Disputing unpaid tax liens can backfire, if the tax authority discovers you are trying to remove it from your credit report.

Negative information pertaining to guaranteed **student loans** can be removed. You must contact the lender of your loan, and request that you intend to rehabilitate the loan. After you make 12 consecutive payments, the negative information should be removed. Although this option is available to student loans that are currently in default, before a default occurs, negotiate with the lender for a deferment, forbearance or graduated payments.

**Step 4: Review Results and Verify Accuracy**

The credit bureau may respond in three different ways.

1.  A new credit report with the results.
    a.  Review your report and make sure the disputed items have been corrected or removed.
2.  A request for more information.
    a.  Just provide the credit bureau with the requested information.
3.  A rejection letter indicating the request was frivolous. This will normally happen if:
    a.  You are disputing too many items in a short period.
    b.  You tell the credit bureaus that you are attempting to repair your credit.
    c.  You are not clear with the items that you are disputing.

If you do not hear from the credit bureaus within 40 days of filing your dispute, send them another letter. Inform them that you requested that inaccurate information be removed 40 days ago, and that you have not received an answer. Include a copy of your return receipt.

If your second dispute letter was ignored, or you received a rejection letter, send a more persuasive letter. At this point, you can inform the credit bureaus that the Fair Credit Reporting Act issues significant fines when a credit bureau mishandles a dispute. Also let the credit bureau know that you are forwarding a copy of this letter to local Federal

Trade Commission (FTC) and your State Attorney
General. The State Attorney General and local
Federal Trade Commission can be found online or
in the telephone book.

## Step 5: Aggressive Verification

The Fair Credit Reporting Act (FCRA) provides many advantages, which will allow you challenge information in your credit report. To download the FCRA go to: www.ftc.gov/os/statutes/fcrajump.shtm. The Fair Credit Reporting Act also protects your rights concerning your personal credit reports. It mandates that credit reporting agencies accurately report information. If information is inaccurate, incomplete, misleading, outdated or unverifiable, that data must be removed.

If negative information in your credit report is verified by the credit bureau(s):
1. Contact the creditor.
2. Inform the creditor that they are reporting inaccurate information to the credit bureaus on your credit report.
3. Inform them that the account is not yours and you want them to mail you written proof and documentation that this is your account. Also, demand that the creditor include a signed written contract with their proof.
4. Tell the creditor they have a week to give you the proof or you will contact the Attorney General.

Creditors and collection agencies store their information in computers. As a result, signed contracts are often unidentifiable or stored in a warehouse. Thus, if the creditor is unable to provide the proof, they must remove the item from your credit report or face significant fines.

5.  If the creditors do not respond in a week, call them again and firmly tell them that they must remove the item from your credit reports or you report them to the Attorney General's Office.
6.  Demand a letter from the creditor indicating that the item has been removed.
7.  If forced verification does not work, you may take your creditors to small claims court.

## Step 6: Negotiate for a Letter of Deletion

Debt remains on your credit reports for seven years from when the account was last active. If you pay off old debt, you can start that seven year clock over again. If left unpaid, tax liens can remain on a credit report for seven years from the date paid or indefinitely. Bankruptcies can stay on your credit report for ten years from the date discharged.

After your creditor provide you with proof of the disputed item, contact the creditor to negotiate the debt. Ask for a supervisor that can authorize a settlement. If you have the money, initially offer a settlement of 15%-45%. If you owe $10,000, offer $2,500. If the creditor refuses, inform them that you are considering bankruptcy and they will receive nothing. If you are persuasive, they will be more willing to settle. Only agree to an amount that you can comfortably pay.

1. Before paying the creditor, make sure the creditor sends you a letter agreeing that they will report to the credit bureaus that the account is paid, never late, and current. Do not pay anything until you receive this letter of deletion.
2. If your account is open, the creditor will normally close your account if you decide to negotiate the debt. Please note that this technique only works on unsecured debt.
3. You should negotiate with the collection company only if the original creditor has charged off the debt.

## Step 7: Repeat the Process

Again, the Fair Credit Reporting Act (FCRA) was designed to protect consumers. You can dispute items on your credit report as many times as you think is necessary. If you remain diligent, sooner or later your creditor will drop the ball and miss the 30 day deadline.

If the credit bureaus claim that they have already verified the information, mail them a certified and return receipt letter reminding them the Fair Credit Reporting Act (FCRA) requires that they verify your disputes and there is a significant fine for each mishandled dispute. Also remind them that part of their 30 day time limit has already expired.

## Make a Comment

According to the Fair Credit Reporting Act (FCRA) you can include a 100-word explanation of negative credit items in your credit report. This explanation will allow anyone who reviews your report to evaluate your side of the story. Your rationalization should something that was out of your control, such as:

1. Medical Issues
2. Layoffs
3. Creditor error

Make sure your explanation is reasonable and has substance. If you need assistance, the FCRA even requires the credit bureau to help you write the 100-word explanation.

## Maximizing Your Credit Score

You should always make sure that your credit score is the best that it can be! Your credit score often determines your life style. While you are building your credit, make sure you:

1. *Pay off or down your open balance.*
2. *Find Creative ways to Pay-off Revolving Balance.*

The first, easiest and fastest way to add established credit to your account is by having your name added as an *authorized user.* This method can immediately boost your credit score. However, if this account is late, it will reflect on your credit report.

Accounts that are older and paid on time have a greater impact on your FICO score. Thus, request the help of only dependable friends or family members that have a credit card, which is at least three years old. Your friend or family member should contact the credit card company and request that you are to be added as an authorized user. The credit card company will generally issue a second credit card in your name. They do not have to worry because the card will be mailed to them. Thus, they can take you off the account at any time without any risk.

A second approach to establish credit is *secured credit cards*. Before obtaining a secured credit card, shop around for the best interest rate and lowest application fee. Although secured credit cards are an easy way to establish credit, it can take six months to improve your credit FICO score. Consider this method as a credit development tool.

With secured credit cards, the bank gives a credit card limit of, for example, $500. In return, you will deposit $500 in the bank for security. The bank will report this account as a normal credit card.

The lower you keep your balance the better your FICO score. Thus, keep your balance below 30% of the balance and make your payments on time. As a result, often, the bank will increase your credit limit.

A third method to reestablish credit is through the use of a *secured loan* at a bank or credit union in your community. Thus, meet with a loan officer and inform him/her that you are trying to reestablish your credit. Tell the officer that you need a short-term loan and intend to deposit $500 as collateral. This is a 100% risk free proposition to the financial institution. Make sure that the bank or credit union in your community reports the loan to the credit bureaus.

Request that the loan term is for only six months to a year. After receiving the loan, take the money to another community bank or credit union and duplicate the process three to four times. After the third or fourth time that you duplicated the process, deposit the cash in a checking account and use it to repay the loans. Write the checks to repay the loans one week earlier than the due date.

A fourth method for reestablishing credit is by opening department store and gas station *retail accounts*. Your FICO score will increase significantly when you charge and pay off the balance consistently.

A fifth method to build your credit score is by requesting that your credit card company *increase your credit score*. A credit card that is 50% or more maxed out is more likely to have a negative impact on your credit. Thus, having your credit limit increased will most likely significantly increase your credit score.

**Discipline and Persistency** will provide you with excellent credit. Follow the prescribed steps and you will have the leverage to move to the next level of financial freedom. Make sure you pull your FICO credit score every six months and repeat the process when necessary.

## Protect Your Identity

After you completely repaired and developed your credit, make sure that you protected from *identity theft*, which consists of five major areas:

1. Driver's license
2. Social Security Numbers
3. Medical Information
4. Character/Criminal actions
5. Financial Transactions

Most companies only protect your financial identity. **For Identity Theft Protection:** www.identity.armcgee.com .

To learn how to save $100(s) to $1000(s) per year on your taxes:
*Email*: info@armlawgroup.com

To **receive updates**, contact the author, submit questions, or provide success *testimonials*
*Email*: info@armlawgroup.com .

Best to you and yours! ☺

**<u>Notes:</u>**

**<u>Notes:</u>**